1

"Your body is a
cradle of love."

"Blossoming with
love and life."

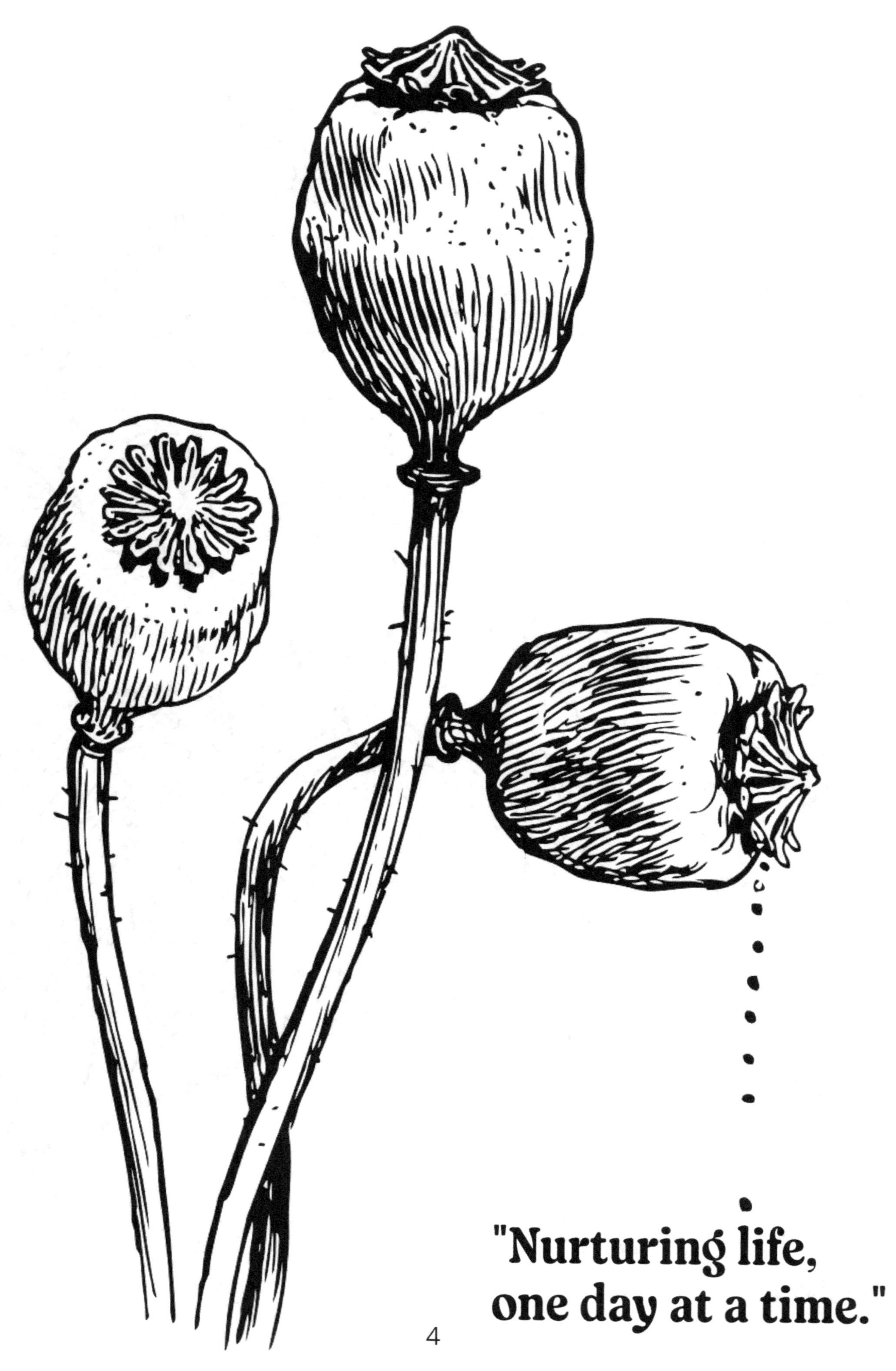

4

"Your body is
creating magic."

"A mother's love
knows no bounds."

"Your love story begins
with two heartbeats."

8

"In the stillness,
find your strength."

"Cherish this
precious time."

10

"Breathe, relax,
and bloom."

"You're nurturing the
world's greatest treasure."

"Your journey is a story
waiting to be colored."

14

"A mother's love
is a work of art."

"A garden of life is
growing within."

"A mother's love,
a baby's first home."

"Whispers of
tiny dreams."

"A mother's journey,
a child's destiny."

20

"Preparing to write
a new chapter."

"Savoring every
kick and flutter."

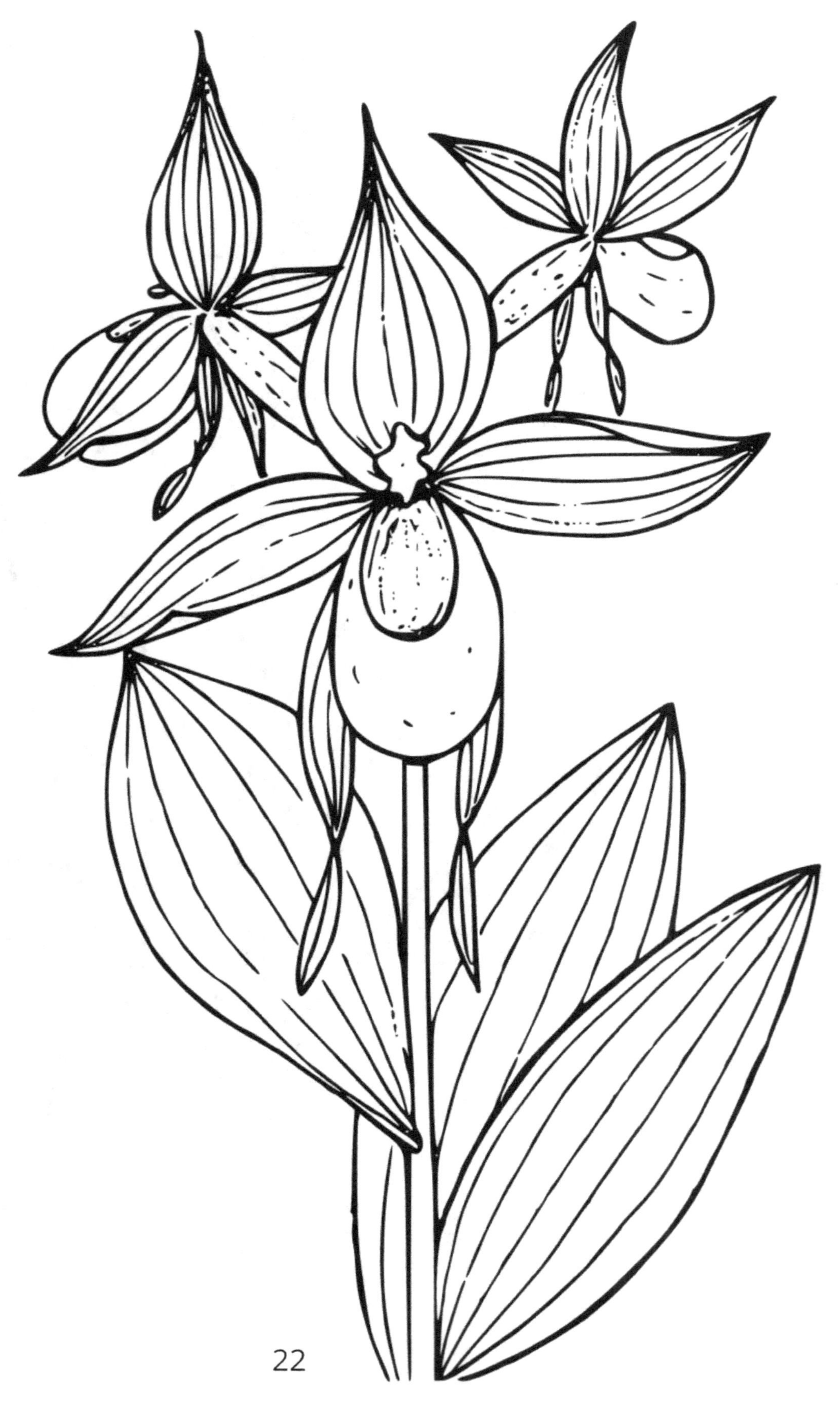

"Growing a
tiny miracle."

" You'll witness a masterpiece soon."

"Infinite love, one
tiny heartbeat."

www.ingramcontent.com/pod-product-compliance
Lightning Source LLC
Chambersburg PA
CBHW080948260726
48661CB00010B/4149